When Your Lover Leaves You

When Your Lover Leaves You

Six Stages to Recovery and Growth

Richard G. Whiteside, M.S.W.
Frances E. Steinberg, Ph.D.

ST. MARTIN'S GRIFFIN ⚑ NEW YORK

www.stmartins.com

Design by Nancy Resnick

Library of Congress Cataloging-in-Publication Data

Whiteside, Richard G.
When your lover leaves you: six stages to recovery and growth / Richard G. Whiteside,
Frances E. Steinberg.
p. cm.
ISBN 0-312-25353-2 (hc)
ISBN 0-312-27279-0 (pbk)
1. Man-woman relationships. 2. Separation (Psychology) 3. Adjustment
(Psychology) 4. Single people—Psychology. I. Steinberg, Frances E., 1951– II.
Title.

HQ801.W67 2000
306.7—dc21   99-055564

D10 9 8 7 6 5 4

In memory of Sam Steinberg,
who at the age of eighty-two was still leaving and loving

Contents

Acknowledgments

The origins of this book began while working with innumerable clients who were frustrated hearing suggestions from well-meaning friends and family such as "time will heal" and "you need to find another lover." These individuals shared both their pain and their secrets of recovery, as they helped us to understand how one can travel from suffering to personal growth. We are indebted to all of the clients who tried out suggestions and let us know what worked and what didn't. Their effort and insight has hopefully created a better book for you.

Thanks also to all of our colleagues who provided feedback, including Suzi Tucker, who gave us helpful ideas during the initial phases of the book. Michael Yapko has been continually generous with his many resources and contacts. Our agent, Audrey Wolf, allowed us to feel as secure as possible through her competent handling of the project, even though we are geographically far away from the action. Lara Asher, our editor at St. Martin's Press, believed in the importance of helping lovers in distress. She has been supportive and positive through some unsettled times.

Rick Whiteside would like to thank his family for showing patience and understanding during his own romantic journeys and upheavals. Frances Steinberg is indebted to Martha Spice and Becky Sparks for holding her hand on the roller coaster.

A final word of thanks to the Slapper, Heartbreak, Michigan, Psycho, and the Nurse, who have made their own unique contributions to the cause.

When Your Lover
Leaves You

Introduction

∽

Melanie could not believe her ears. Mike, the man she had shared her life with for almost three years, was telling her that their relationship was over. It just didn't make sense. Only last month they had made plans to pool their resources and move in together. They wanted to have a small apartment in the city for when they worked during the week and a tiny cabin in the woods for weekends. How could Mike, who constantly told her that she was the partner he had always searched for, now be saying that he wanted to leave?

Melanie had noticed changes in his behavior over the past month but thought that he was simply stressed from work. And then tonight Mike told her that he was confused about their relationship and needed some time to sort through his feelings. He said that he loved her but was feeling bored and restless. Mike rambled on about his needs and his desire to explore other facets of his life. Confused and upset, Melanie finally realized that what Mike really wanted was to end their relationship. Too devastated to talk, she tried to listen while he explained that the problem had nothing to do with her; it came from inside of him. By the time he left, Melanie felt completely dazed.

Sound familiar? The above scenario is typical of how many relationships end. Confusion, ambivalence, disappointment, and pain now fill the spaces that had previously been full of love and tenderness. Anger and bitterness replace warmth and understanding. Plans dissolve, and all the familiar aspects of life take on an unknown quality.

When relationships end, they cause emotional trauma and disrupt daily functioning. Our normal reactions to things elude us and are replaced with strange and unfamiliar behaviors. But the emotions and reactions that we feel after the termination of a relationship often follow a predictable pattern, a series of stages that eventually lead to healing. This book is a guide to those stages and the feelings that accompany them. It will help you understand what you are experiencing and provide you with concrete strategies to help your passage through each phase.

Six Stages to Personal Growth

The typical pattern that adults follow after the termination of a relationship is divided into six stages:

- **Shock**—Disbelief and numbness, marked by difficulty with eating, sleeping, and general functioning.

- **Hope**—Active attempts, negotiations, and manipulations designed to try and win the lover back.
- **Anger**—Outward expressions of animosity directed toward the lover.
- **Despair**—Inward direction of emotions, including depression and self-doubt.
- **Indifference**—No significant emotional response to lover.
- **Growth**—Feelings expressed in a positive way and transferred to a new relationship.

Although the order presented above is by far the most common, each person's path through the stages is different. Some people skip certain stages altogether; others spend more time in one and less in another. For example, you may find that you never experience despair or that you spend a minimal amount of time in shock. Or you may enter the despair stage before, rather than after, you become angry. There is no right or wrong order, only a pattern that is more or less typical.

Sometimes your personality or past experiences determine the amount of time you spend in a particular stage. For instance, if you are aggressive and outgoing, you might enter the anger stage right away and not pass out of it easily. Or, if you have a history of bad relationships, you will have a greater tendency to become fixated in the despair stage. If you are a take-charge, analytical person, you could remain in the hope stage longer, believing that you have the ability to problem-solve the issues away.

The pattern and duration of your particular reactions

can also be affected by the length of time you have spent in a relationship. Couples in long-term relationships have a substantial history of shared intimacies, goals, friends, and aspirations, and the disruption of their bond has wide-ranging ramifications that often lead to prolonged time in the shock and despair stages. The termination of short-term relationships also can be extremely painful because the level of emotion and passion is running high prior to the breakup, leading to a possible fixation in the anger stage.

Unfortunately, there are no magical timetables to let us know when we are beginning to fixate in a particular stage. Generally, the amount of time spent in the shock stage should be the shortest, because the body can not handle that state for very long. The amount of time you spend in other stages will be a product of your personality, your past history with relationships, the nature and length of the relationship that just terminated, and the way in which it ended.

The important thing to remember is that all of the reactions following the termination of a relationship are normal. Be accepting of your emotional responses, knowing that each stage is a reasonable result of what has happened to you and an important part of your healing. No stage is inherently good or bad. Don't feel that anger and despair are negative and indifference and growth are positive—all of the stages serve a purpose. Validate your feelings while you have them and accept that they are a part of the process, but don't wallow in them. Problems result when individuals become stuck in a particular phase and are unable to move out of it. By passing through the stages, you can make the transition from pain to potential.

Our Reactions Stem from Childhood

When a lover leaves, we experience strange feelings and often do things we never would have dreamed of before the relationship ended. Our emotions, our actions, and even our bodies seem foreign to us, almost as if we were taken over by some alien being.

Many psychologists and psychiatrists believe that the reactions to being left by a lover are related to biologically programmed behaviors present in infancy. Early in life we make our first commitments; we learn to trust the people taking care of us and give them our love in return. If for some reason a child is separated from a caregiver, a typical reaction pattern occurs. First, he or she enters into a "protest" phase. The child cries, screams, runs after his or her caregiver—in short, does anything to try to reestablish contact. All the child knows is that the person who provided love and protection is gone and needs to be found.

If the protest fails and the separation continues, the child generally enters into a "despair" phase. Eating is poor, sleeping difficult, and the child generally mopes around all the time, acting very depressed. Nothing is of interest, not toys, not people. Life doesn't seem worth living if the child can't be with the one he or she loves.

If the child is then reunited with his or her caregiver, or if patient, loving intervention occurs during the separation, the child can come out of the despair stage and resume positive relationships with others. If, however, the separation is permanent or if the child has no support during his or her suffering, he or she may enter a "detachment" phase. While the child appears to be better on the surface—he or she is now eating, sleeping, playing—close examination reveals that the child does not allow others to get close and no longer forms any emotional connections. The child has sealed off rejection and cauterized pain by refusing to risk getting hurt again. Because the child does not form any more emotional attachments, he or she doesn't have to worry about rejection or abandonment.

Adult reactions strongly parallel those seen in childhood. Your lover leaves you and your initial reactions are remarkably similar to those of a child in the protest stage—you cry, scream, and run after him or her, trying anything you can to make your lover come back to you. When this doesn't work, depression sets in—you have trouble eating and sleeping, and nothing really interests you. Eventually the depression lessens, and you either make the transition to healthy independence and the ability to form new relationships or you seal off your emotions, determined not to get hurt again.

However, adults are considerably more complex than children and have a greater range of analytical and emotional responses, not to mention a substantial history of positive and negative relationships. Our passage through the stages after separation are often more complicated than a child's, and the amount of time we spend at any stage, and the order we go through them, depends upon our individual personalities and the previous experiences we have had. Adults also have a wider range of resources for resolving their difficulties.

Solutions

It's one thing to understand what's happening to you; it's quite another to be able to do something concrete about it. Everyone around you has advice, although most of it sounds the same—"You need to find someone else," "Time will heal the pain," "Accept what happened and move on," or "You're better off without that jerk anyway."

While many of these suggestions have an element of truth, it doesn't help to hear them while you're suffering, especially if they don't fit the emotions you're experiencing at the current stage. In fact, it often seems that the more "help" you get, the worse you feel, and your friends' well-meaning advice starts to sound cold or irritating.

There are, however, things you can do to ease your pain and make life more bearable. The most useful way of doing this is to match the stage you are in with the steps you need to take, realizing that the advice for getting through despair would not be helpful during shock. Suggestions need to fit your current emotional state and level of energy, otherwise they seem hurtful or annoying.

Each chapter in the book describes one of the six stages a person goes through when his or her lover leaves and then gives practical suggestions on how to deal with the issues present at that time. You can easily choose which techniques might be right for you and the feelings you are having at any particular time. By following the strategies, you can deal with the problems inherent to the stage you're in and work to make the transition to the next phase.

Read the whole book from beginning to end the first time through. After you finish, return to the section that most appropriately describes what you are currently experiencing. Re-read the description of that stage and then the solutions presented. Find one of the strategies that appeals to you and try it. You don't need to do all of the suggestions at once or in the order presented. Use the ones with which you feel comfortable and do only as many as you can handle.

You will find after doing particular exercises that at some point they don't seem appropriate anymore. Chances are you have shifted to another stage. Find the one that matches your issues at the current time and repeat the process.

"Should-ers"

When you feel unhappy, it helps to get support and love from others. Friends and family can offer real comfort, giving you affection at a time when you feel abandoned and alone. Be wary, however, of the shoulder to cry on that turns into a "should-er," someone who tells you how you should or should not behave or feel. In your pain, you are susceptible to other people's opinions and are worried about having their approval. Often you want to please them by doing what they suggest, even if it doesn't seem right to you.

"Shoulds" are counterproductive to healing, especially if they don't match how you feel. Many times people tell you things that you know are "right" or worthwhile, but you just can't seem to put them into action. Not being able to follow through on their suggestions makes you feel even more miserable. It may be, however, that it is the right advice but the wrong time for it. The ideas they give you might not be appropriate for the stage you're in. Thank them for their suggestion and tell them you will file it away to use when you're ready for it.

While you're at it, make sure that you don't give yourself a list of "shoulds" either.

✍

Don't Judge Yourself; Don't Let Others Judge You.

✍

BE YOUR OWN BEST FRIEND.

At each stage it is important to be gentle with yourself. Don't chastise yourself for not getting better immediately. Your body and spirit need to grieve, need to get angry, and then need to get better. Be as kind and understanding with yourself as you would be with a friend or family member. Don't expect instant results or get impatient when you don't progress as quickly as you want. Keep working on your healing, and you will get better in a way that works for you.

On the other hand, if no matter how hard you try, you

seem to be stuck in a particular stage for an extended period of time, you may need outside help. Start by asking for feedback from a friend or family member. What may seem to you like an eternity spent in one stage might actually be a fairly brief time. If he or she agrees that you have become immobilized despite your best efforts, you may want to seek assistance from a counselor or therapist.

By all means, if you feel extremely desperate, despondent, or suicidal, make sure you get professional help. Don't let things get so far out of control that your options seem nonexistent. This isn't a sign of weakness. It is a mark of exceptional personal strength to ask for help when it's needed.

Typical Reaction Patterns

We'd like to close this section with two interviews, one with a woman, the other with a man, whose lovers have left them. The patterns of reaction they describe are typical of those of many others with whom we have worked or interviewed and are good examples of the stages listed above.

CLARA AND PARKER

The first interview is with Clara, a thirty-three-year-old accountant, who became involved with her lover shortly after her divorce.

INTERVIEWER: How did your relationship begin?

CLARA: I was a student in Parker's aerobics class. I was married when I first started classes there. Parker wasn't; he's never been married. He was always a flirt, you know, constantly coming on to the women in the class. I used to watch it and laugh, the way he would pursue one student after another. When a mutual friend told him that my marriage was over, Parker started flirting with me. He was really different from anyone I had ever been involved with. I was always so intellectual, and he was more into physical things. It was like one of those fantasy relationships out of a soap opera or a romance novel, with the down-and-dirty guy and the aloof, proper woman. I don't know if I really trusted him, but he was so passionate, it was kind of overwhelming and flattering.

Anyway, we got involved. After six months of dating and seeing each other, we decided he'd move into my house. Things were very romantic and highly charged in a sexual way. It was different from my marriage, which had been much less passionate.

INTERVIEWER: When did you first notice things weren't going so well?

CLARA: There were some small signs, starting a few months after he moved in. Parker asked me not to come to certain classes he was teaching. He said that I was too "distracting" to have there. And at times it seemed like he wasn't paying attention to what I was saying. One time we bumped into some friends of mine from work that Parker didn't know, and he stood off to the side. He didn't want to talk to them or meet them. Even so, there was still a strong connection between us. He was very demonstrative, very vocal about how he felt about me.

INTERVIEWER: What finally happened?

CLARA: Well, one day I came home and started to make dinner. Parker wasn't there, but he had a fairly weird schedule, so that wasn't unusual. The phone rang. It was Parker, asking if I was upset. I had no idea what he was talking about. After a few minutes it became more clear. He said he had left me a note and the key to the house on the dining room table, but I hadn't seen them when I came in, I had gone straight to the kitchen with the groceries. He kept talking to me, telling me he wasn't sure about what he was doing, saying that he was confused, that he still wanted to be with me, he just needed some space so that he could work things out in his own head.

INTERVIEWER: How did you feel?

CLARA: Actually I didn't. I felt numb, like I was in a daze. I knew he was talking to me, but nothing made sense. This was the same guy who, the night before, went on and on about how I made his whole life better. When I hung up the phone, I walked in and read the note, but I didn't really see what it said. By the time I looked around the house and saw that all of his things were gone—he must have taken them while I was at work—I was in total shock. I remember sitting on the bed and crying for a while. Then I called my friend Rachel. She came over and talked with me. I was pretty upset, but I felt too numb to cry. After she left, I fell apart, crying and beating the pillow. Parker called fairly late, said he was just checking to see if I was okay, that he really cared about me.

INTERVIEWER: How did you react to that?

CLARA: I think his call, and the way he spoke to me, made me feel like everything that happened was a mistake, that he really still loved me but was just having some personal problems. I think I felt that if I gave him some space living away from me, he would begin to appreciate me again.

INTERVIEWER: Did you just leave him alone then?

CLARA: (laughing) God, no. If anything, I probably was more involved with him then than I had ever been when we were living together. I would call all the time. Most of the time I got his answering machine, so I would leave him these cute little messages. I still went to classes, and Parker would be really sweet to me there. I made it a point to clean up the room for him after class and made sure that all of his equipment was in order. I sent him flowers and cards and little notes all the time. We would spend the night together about two times a week. I had this sense that things would be all right again in time.

INTERVIEWER: But they weren't?

CLARA: No. Every once in a while I would sort of put out a feeler, ask Parker how he felt about me, about us. He would get angry, say that I was pressuring him like I used to. He wouldn't call for a week or so, which devastated me. I would call, but Parker never answered his phone. I stopped by his apartment one day to drop off a card. A young woman answered his door when I knocked and told me Parker wasn't there, but she would give him the card. In my state, it never even occurred to me that he might be involved with her. I came up with all of these other reasons why she might be there.

INTERVIEWER: How did you realize that things weren't how you wanted them?

CLARA: It was my thirtieth birthday. Parker was supposed to come over to see me, but he didn't show up. I began to get worried about him, kept calling him, his friends, his family, but nobody had seen him. At about eleven o'clock I went over to his apartment. I was knocking on the door, crying, but nobody answered. I was frantic. I drove around to the parking lot of this fast food place where I had a view of his door and parked. I sat in the car and watched his door. It was cold out, so every once in a while, I turned on the heater and warmed the car up.

By two in the morning, he still hadn't come home. I was cold, tired, and crazy by then. All of a sudden, these lights came on, blinding me, and I heard a voice on a bullhorn tell me to come out of the car with my hands up. I was stunned. I got out of the car slowly with my hands up. There must have been four police cars there, officers with guns. The police relaxed when they saw me—I think it was my rainbow mittens that assured them. I told them I had been worried about a friend who hadn't come home, that she had been on a date with a weird guy, and I was watching for her because she hadn't answered her phone. The police said they had been called by the fast food place, who had been sure I was there casing the place before I robbed them. I was beyond shaken. I went home and got hysterical. I think it was such a bizarre experience that I realized how stupid I'd been behaving, groveling after him like that. It put everything into perspective for me.

INTERVIEWER: Did it change how you felt about him? How you acted?

CLARA: I think I got really angry. I realized he had been using me, that he never had any intention of coming back, that all of that had been a bunch of bullshit. I was furious with him.

INTERVIEWER: What did you do?

CLARA: I stopped going to his classes at that point. I think I also started bad-mouthing Parker to women I knew who went there. All someone had to do was mention his name, and I'd be off on a tirade. I refused to talk to him if he called. One time, I picked up the phone while he was leaving this sweet message on my machine. I think he was really shocked at the way I started screaming at him.

INTERVIEWER: Was that the end of things?

CLARA: Well, he didn't call again. I went through a really bad time for a while once I calmed down. I felt like such an idiot. I should have seen him for what he was. I knew he was a womanizer; I'd watched him for years. I guess I had thought that I would be the one to make him settle down. I got fairly depressed. I remember that New Year's Eve was coming up. It was the first time since junior high that I didn't have someone special to share it with. I was feeling pretty low and toyed with the idea of calling Parker.

INTERVIEWER: Did you call?

CLARA: No, I called some of my friends instead and we arranged to go skiing over the holiday. I still felt lousy on New Year's—I can remember lying in bed and crying out for Parker. I was lonely and felt really down on myself.

INTERVIEWER: Did the feelings last long? What did you do to get out of it?

CLARA: I can remember feeling bad for a few months. There'd be things that would remind me of him. Plus I think my body was getting run down since I wasn't exercising as much. I started running, and I joined a yoga class with a woman teacher. She was wonderful, very spiritual and uplifting. I had a new project starting at work, and I threw myself into it. I started feeling better physically and mentally, and the emotional roller-coaster began to subside a little.

INTERVIEWER: Have you had any relationships since then?

CLARA: I went a little wild for a short time. I guess I needed to think I was still attractive, after what happened with my divorce and then Parker. It was a lot of fun, actually, but I got tired of it. A few months ago, I met this guy at a party, and we've been going out exclusively since then.

INTERVIEWER: Do you find yourself behaving differently than you did with Parker?

CLARA: The relationship is a lot more balanced, more grounded. I think I've become more comfortable with myself, with living alone, and it carried over into this relationship. I don't feel like I'm pressing right now. I can just take things as they happen.

Clara's interview demonstrates how she passed through shock, hope, anger, despair, and indifference before she achieved personal and interpersonal growth.

JIM AND TRACIE

The pattern of stages is also reflected in the following interview with Jim, a twenty-nine-year-old salesman, whose termination of a relationship disrupted many phases of his life.

INTERVIEWER: How did your relationship begin?

JIM: Tracie and I went to the same church. I had moved to the area about six months before we met, because there were more sales-type jobs available. I started working for a company selling advertising space; the pay was terrible and they gave you no real contacts, but I figured I would do it until I found something else. I used to see Tracie on Sundays—she was usually at church with her two children and her parents.

One week, I went over to talk to her after the service. Her parents heard that I was new in town and invited me to dinner. I really enjoyed being at their home, coming from a big family myself.

INTERVIEWER: Did you start going out after that?

JIM: I called to thank Tracie's parents for dinner, and they "casually" mentioned that they would be glad to watch the kids if Tracie and I ever wanted to go out. Despite the not-too-subtle hint, I called Tracie and we began seeing each other. We really enjoyed each other's company, and I hit it off with her children. It was great for me in a lot of ways; I guess I didn't realize how much I had missed my family since my move.

INTERVIEWER: Where did things go from there?

JIM: Tracie and I dated for over a year. I was anxious to take things further. I really wanted to get married, but Tracie felt like she had just come out of a bad marriage and wanted to take her time. She said she loved me, and she knew that her kids and I loved each other, but she just wasn't ready for marriage again. I could understand, I guess, because her ex-husband had run out on her and the children. I was willing to wait. I felt like I was part of the family anyway. Her father had seen how miserable I was in my job. He owned a printing company, and he hired me to do his sales work. We worked really well together.

Things went on that way for over four years. Tracie was finally coming around to where she would discuss getting married. Her father took me in as a partner in the company. We discussed my adopting the kids after we got married. I called Tracie from work one day, and she was crying, but she wouldn't tell me what was wrong. I rushed over to her house and rang the bell, but she wouldn't answer the door. I could hear her crying inside, so I got really frantic and started pounding on the door and screaming for her to open up. She finally did let me in. I was sure she had been raped or attacked or something, or that one of the kids had been hurt. Tracie told me to come in and sit down, that she had something to tell me. She said that she had recently heard from her ex-husband, that he wanted to patch things up with her and start being a father to their children. Tracie said that he had changed, he was more like the man she had first married. He was the father of her children, and he had some rights.

INTERVIEWER: What did you say?

JIM: I don't think I could even speak for the first few minutes. My heart was pounding so fast that I thought I was going to pass out. When I could finally talk, I told her how much I loved her, that we had plans, that she knew that I was stable and reliable, and that I would be a better husband and father than this guy could ever be.

INTERVIEWER: Was she convinced?

JIM: Tracie started to cry again, and said that she had given this a lot of thought, and that even though she loved me, she also still had feelings for him, and that if he had changed, she owed it to her children to try and set things right.

INTERVIEWER: What did you do?

JIM: I finally left. I agreed to give her some time to try and work this out. I couldn't go back to work, partly because I felt sick and partly because I couldn't face her father right then. I think I went home and tried to watch a football game, but all I could do was go over our conversation in my head again and again.

INTERVIEWER: Then what happened?

JIM: I was still really upset the next day, but I went to work. Tracie's father came in to talk to me, and he was pretty upset himself. He disliked her ex-husband intensely for what he had done to Tracie and his grandchildren and couldn't understand what she was doing. We commiserated with each other for a while, and he convinced me that this could never work out, that this guy could never keep it together.

INTERVIEWER: So what did you do?

JIM: I tried to show Tracie that I was a better man than her ex-husband. I sent her flowers and balloons with cards to tell her how much I missed her. I even offered to watch the kids for her anytime she wanted to go out. I would call her on the phone and listen while she told me how things were going, just to show her that I was an understanding guy.

INTERVIEWER: Did your plan work?

JIM: Well, I guess it worked out for her. It turns out that she used the time when I watched the kids to spend lots of time with him, enough for her to realize she wanted to go back to him. She decided to take the kids and move to the neighboring town where this guy had a house.

INTERVIEWER: How did you feel?

JIM: I felt like such a jerk! I was furious. I felt like she had used me to get him back. I was so angry that I went to her new house, and when she wouldn't open the door, I threw a rock through her window before I left. I couldn't believe I had done that, but I had never felt so angry in my life. When she sent me a bill for the window, I ripped it up into about a hundred pieces.

INTERVIEWER: Did the anger help?

JIM: No, it didn't. As a matter of fact it made things a lot worse. Tracie's father heard what I had done, and he called me into his office. He said that I knew that he didn't approve of Tracie's behavior, but that he couldn't condone what I had done. He said that maybe I had better look for somewhere else to work, because he wasn't sure that it would work out with me here.

INTERVIEWER: What did you do?

JIM: I really fell apart. It was bad enough losing Tracie, but I also lost her kids, the contact with her family, and then my job. I hated myself for what I had done, but I knew apologizing wouldn't fix anything that really mattered. It wouldn't bring Tracie back. I was isolated from everything I cared about and embarrassed by my behavior. I felt really worthless and alone, and I didn't trust myself. I couldn't sleep, and I couldn't find the energy to look for another job. I finally applied for a job at a car dealership, but I hated the work, and being friendly to the customers at that time in my life was very difficult.

INTERVIEWER: How did you snap out of this?

JIM: One of my brothers came to the rescue. He called and said that he was interested in buying a franchise restaurant, but that he needed some help in setting it up. He asked me to move back to my hometown and give him a hand. I turned him down at first, but then I realized that it was the most sensible thing to do. I would have some challenging work, and I would be in a place where I had family again. I was shaky at first, but I received a lot of love and support from my family.

INTERVIEWER: Did you ever contact Tracie again?

JIM: About a year after this whole thing happened, we needed some printing done at work. I knew that Tracie's father would do the job better and cheaper than any of the other places we had received quotes from. I called him, and we spoke. I thanked him for all of the help and kindness he had shown me over the years. He told me that things hadn't worked out with Tracie and her ex-husband and asked me if I wanted her to call. I thought about it briefly, but I realized that I wanted all of that behind me, and I really didn't care to start it up again. I told him to say hello to the kids for me. When I hung up, it hit me how much better I was doing. I could reflect back on the situation, but I didn't feel hurt from it.

INTERVIEWER: Are you in a relationship now?

JIM: No. For the time being I'm enjoying getting my business established and being with my family. I feel like if the right person comes along, I'll notice, but I don't feel like going out and looking for someone at this point.

The termination of Jim's relationship caused repercussions in many areas of his life. Endings often mean that our typical ways of behaving, and even our daily habits, are disrupted. You can feel uncomfortable around friends or family you shared with your lover. Even a meal at a favorite restaurant can be traumatic, as you experience painful memories or worry about the appearance of your ex-lover. But like Jim and Clara from the previous interviews, you'll see that things can get resolved, and once you pass through a series of reactions, you can come to terms with both the relationship and yourself.

1

Shock

Your lover has just told you the relationship is over. Even if you had noticed a deterioration in the relationship, the finality of this message hits you like a blow. You feel your senses and mind shutting down, becoming numb in an effort to avoid any unwanted feelings or sensations.

What you are sensing is shock, a physiological reaction built into the body to help it in times of extreme stress or injury. When the body enters shock, it closes down all systems not needed for basic survival. The reaction is designed to protect you, to keep the body alive and sealed off from pain. Normal functioning is impossible because the body shuts down. Thinking gets clouded and reasoning becomes difficult because of the changes in the physiological system.

Shock often sets in when your lover terminates a relationship, and you experience a general disruption of reality.

Over time you built up expectations and developed an understanding of your relationship and your lover. Suddenly, nothing makes sense. The facts you have just received about your lover's feelings don't fit into your previous frame of reference. You've landed in the Twilight Zone.

Your body and mind become numb in an effort to block out the pain and ease the confusion. Denial seems preferable to facing reality. Eating and sleeping are often poor, and it is extremely difficult to concentrate on anything at all. Going to work becomes an ordeal. You often feel physically ill. Your emotional haze is frequently disrupted with bursts of hysteria. You experience shock as clearly as if you had suffered a physical, and not an emotional, accident.

Consider the reaction of Barbara, a twenty-eight-year-old physical therapist, after her lover, Nick, terminated their relationship.

INTERVIEWER: How did your relationship begin?
BARBARA: We met at a professional meeting—we're both physical therapists. Nick and I were sitting next to each other at lunch. There was a strong physical attraction, and he kept flirting with me. He asked me out to dinner after the meeting. Our relationship developed after that, I guess. We got together and dated a few times. Nick was incredibly thoughtful, sweet. Most of the guys I had been involved with before were really macho, so Nick was a nice change. We had a lot in common professionally, which was also a plus. We even talked about going into practice together. Things gradually became more serious, and

we started seeing each other exclusively. It was a comfortable relationship, but we also had a lot of passion. Over a three-year period we became a couple and developed mutual friends and mutual lives.

INTERVIEWER: What changed?

BARBARA: One night, we went out to dinner and saw a movie. Afterwards, we came back to my house, and I got us something to drink. When I sat down next to Nick, he turned to me and said, "I've decided to move to Oregon." Just like that, real direct and matter of fact. I didn't know what to say to him.

INTERVIEWER: How did you feel?

BARBARA: Like I had been hit over the head. I didn't know what to say. Finally I think I said something like "What about me?"

INTERVIEWER: How did Nick respond to that?

BARBARA: He hugged me and told me how much he loved me. He said that he was just sick of the East Coast, that this had nothing to do with me. In fact, he would be thrilled if I went with him, we could move out there together. I felt really confused, it was all so sudden. Then he told me it was all arranged, that he would be leaving in two weeks, that he already had a job and needed to be at work within the month. I started to cry. Nick was really gentle, soothing me, telling me how much he loved me and hoped that I would come with him. When he left, I sat there like I had been shot.

INTERVIEWER: What bothered you the most?

BARBARA: I think that he had made all of his plans without talking to me first. No matter how much he said that he wanted me to come, it seemed like I was irrelevant in his decision. That message, that pain, just stuck in me and really hurt. How could he have made plans without me if I was so important to him?

INTERVIEWER: What did you do?

BARBARA: The first day or so was really painful. I felt confused, really in a daze. I called a few of my friends, but they weren't much help. They either told me what a shit Nick was for doing this or lectured me about going to Oregon. None of that was really helpful; it just made the pain worse. I couldn't eat right, and I wasn't sleeping. I kept thinking about our plans—how they had changed. Nick was really sweet whenever I spoke to him, but I didn't trust him completely anymore. No matter how many times he said that he wanted me to come with him, something inside me would scream, "But you made the plans without me." I was miserable.

Barbara's first reaction to Nick's news was one of shock. She couldn't think straight, eat or sleep properly, or listen to her friends' advice. Shock might be designed to protect the body, but it is very disruptive in the process.

Remember—
If you feel desperate or suicidal, contact someone—a crisis line, a therapist, a friend, or family
member.

Ask for help. Don't try to tough things out on your
own because you feel that asking for assistance
would be a sign of weakness or an imposition.

Get help if you need it!

Strategies for the Shock Stage

While it is unrealistic to expect yourself to behave nor-
mally when you are in shock, any more than you would
think a car accident victim should act as if nothing had
happened, you also need to take steps to lessen your distress. This is not the time for difficult work or extensive
analysis. All of that can be dealt with more effectively
once things have normalized and you're thinking more
clearly. Your primary goals for this stage should be:

℘

Feel Comforted and Protected.

Restore the Body and Mind to a More Functional Level.

℘

There are a number of ways that you can accomplish these goals.

KEEP THINGS IN YOUR LIFE AS CONCRETE AS POSSIBLE.

Concentrate on getting your basic needs fulfilled—food, water, sleep, comfort. Now is not the time for self-analysis or intense contemplation but for getting your body functioning again. You'll be able to think much more clearly during some of the later stages.

Make the foods that you eat as nourishing as possible. This is extremely important since the amount that you eat will probably be atypical. Some people react to stress by losing their appetite, others by bingeing. Either way, it is important to make sure that your food intake is nutritious. That way if you can eat only a small amount, your body will still get nourished, and if you overeat, it won't be so hazardous to your health. Complex carbohydrates such as rice, fruit, potatoes, and vegetables tend to have more of a calming effect on the body than sugar, protein, or caffeine. Avoid excessive amounts of alcohol since it will only prolong the haze and numb the senses further.

But now is not the time to make radical changes in your usual habits, either. You don't need to eliminate drinking or cigarettes, just try not to indulge more than usual. The more normal you can make your actions, the faster the shock will pass.

TAKE SMALL STEPS TOWARD FEELING BETTER.

Don't expect to recover completely in a day. As we said earlier, it's important to be gentle and patient with yourself. At the same time, you want to work toward feeling better. Remember that this sense of shock is a physiological reaction that is more out of your conscious control than you'd like.

It helps to pick one small goal that you think you can achieve, even if it's something as basic as not crying for a ten-minute space. Focus on simple things such as eating a set amount of food or being able to do a modest task for work.

By concentrating on small victories, you begin to take back control of your body and your mind. Don't ask yourself to do too much. Find a task that you *know* you can achieve. When you successfully accomplish one goal, it will give you the confidence to try another.

Remember, the overall strategies for this stage are to help yourself feel comforted and protected, and to help your body and mind return to normal functioning. Try to eat better, sleep better, think better—but not all at once.

SURROUND YOURSELF WITH
FRIENDS AND FAMILY.

It feels good to be in the presence of those who still love and value you as a person. Allow them to nurture you, even to spoil you. You don't have to be strong and independent at this point. If you were ill, you'd let them take care of you. Accept their love and concern.

Try not to get into complicated discussions about what happened or the reasons things didn't work out, even though this may be a natural inclination. Use your friends and family to vent your feelings, but save the dissection and analysis for the following stages when your mind is working better.

Should-er alert!! Let family and friends nurture you, but make sure you shy away from any judgmental conversations or remarks from them such as "I told you not to get involved with that jerk" or "You really need to process this and move on." Tell them that you appreciate their opinions but that you're not ready for discussions at this time. If they can't contain themselves enough to stop their lecturing, find someone to console you who is less disruptive. It's important that the people you vent to are emotionally solid themselves—you don't need their neuroses on top of your own pain!

LET PEOPLE AT WORK KNOW THAT YOU ARE GOING THROUGH A DIFFICULT TIME.

You don't have to give the people you work with all the gruesome details, but it might be helpful to let them know you've had an upheaval in your personal life, as you would if you had a death in the family. If you have a boss or supervisor, approach her and tell her that you just ended an important relationship. Acknowledge that your productivity might not be at its best right now. Ask her to inform you when she notices things not getting done or if your work is not up to par. You will usually receive a more compassionate response if you enlist her help rather than try to hide your poor performance.

If you can't talk to your employer, pick a colleague who can act as a monitor for you, to watch your work and cover your back. While you may feel embarrassed admitting that you're having personal problems to a colleague, it beats being fired.

Don't force yourself to sleep if you can't.

It's natural if you find yourself sleeping more than usual just after a relationship termination—sleep restores the body and offers space and relief from thinking about what happened. However, after a day or two of excessive sleep, you should enter into a more normal pattern. If you are still oversleeping past this time, consider whether you are using sleep to avoid dealing with your situation.

If, on the other hand, you find you are having trouble sleeping, listen to some soothing music or take a hot bath. If neither of these works for you, try some relaxation exercises.

- Meditate instead of sleep. One simple method is to lie down and focus on counting your breaths. Count how long it takes you to breathe in. Try and hold your breath for two counts longer than you inhaled, and breathe out for two counts longer than you held your breath. For example, count to two when you breathe in. Inhale—1, 2. Then hold your breath for a count of four—1, 2, 3, 4—before you breathe out for a count of six—1, 2, 3, 4, 5, 6. Repeat the entire process. In—1, 2. Hold—1, 2, 3, 4. Out—1, 2, 3, 4, 5, 6. Soon you'll find that by concentrating on the breathing and the counting, you begin to feel more relaxed and less stressed.

- If counting doesn't work for you, try visualizing that you are floating on a relaxing cloud. Imagine that you are not lying on your bed but on a cloud of your favorite color. As you breathe, the cloud becomes lighter and fluffier. Feel it holding and comforting you as you float within it. The cloud is softer than your bed and your body becomes light and carefree, moving within the floating motion. Sleep becomes unimportant because you are so comfortable floating on the cloud that your body becomes relaxed and calm. All of the pain and anxiety starts flowing out of your body, seeping into the cloud, leaving you feeling free and serene.

Don't worry if you aren't successful with either the counting or the cloud. Now is not the time to worry about anything or to judge yourself harshly. These things take practice, and they might not be the right drill for you at this time. Like everything else at this stage, use it only if it makes you feel comforted and relaxed.

If none of these methods helps you to sleep, stop struggling and instead find something else to do. Try getting up and writing. Jot down feelings in a journal, compose poetry, or write a letter to a friend. Catch up on some school or office work. It may help you feel productive or just might bore you back to sleep!

CALL YOUR LOVER IF YOU CAN'T
RESIST THE TEMPTATION TO CALL.

Calling your lover is probably not a great idea at this time. The hurt is still fresh and you're not thinking clearly. Some people find, however, that they can't stop thinking about calling their lover. If that is the case, and you feel you must call, go ahead. At a later point you will be able to refrain from phoning. It's not that calling your lover actually helps you—the conversation can often be painful—but sometimes it's wiser to phone than to think about doing it all day long. If you decide you must call, first try:

- Phoning a friend.
- Making some bread—the length of time it takes you to do it and the physical act of kneading the dough may help you change your mind.
- Planning the conversation. Don't spend the time crying. Instead, ask questions that have been haunting you. For instance, you may want to hear again the exact reason why the person decided to terminate the relationship. Be direct with your questions and ask for specific responses.

TUNE BACK INTO YOUR SENSES.

Shock often closes us off from simple sensory experiences, making the world around us seem fuzzy and gray. One of the simplest ways of reversing the process is to become more aware of the surrounding environment.

- Don't just eat and drink, but experience the meal. Concentrate on how things smell or taste. Focus on the texture and color of the food. Inhale aromas deeply and enjoy special flavors. If you have a favorite wine, savor its bouquet and the way it feels in your mouth.
- Take yourself to places that are interesting from a sensory point of view—the mountains, a museum, a concert, a garden. Think about the different sights, sounds, and smells around you.
- Play your favorite music on the stereo. Indulge yourself with songs that really appeal to you, and avoid those tunes that have special meanings for you and your ex-lover. In fact, why not play all those songs that you love but he or she hated!
- Don't just throw on clothes in the morning. Focus on the colors and textures of what you are going to wear. Feel how smooth or rough an article of clothing feels.
- Take a nice relaxing bath and place some non-staining food coloring or drops of your favorite scent in your bathwater.

Passing Through the Shock Stage

The suggestions offered in the preceding section are all designed to reduce the debilitating sensations of shock and restore normal functioning. Consider how they worked for Philip, a twenty-seven-year-old auto technician after his girlfriend, Meredith, terminated their relationship.

Philip sat staring into space. The air around him seemed fuzzy and cloudy. He could see that Meredith's mouth was moving, but he really hadn't heard anything past when she said that she wanted to stop seeing him because she was interested in a guy from work. Philip's mind was reeling. He and Meredith were supposed to go to Jamaica next week—they had planned the trip for a year. Not wanting to make a scene in the restaurant, Philip excused himself from the table. By the time he got out the door, his chest was aching and his ears ringing.

Philip managed to get home and flop down on the bed. When the phone rang a short while later, he grabbed it, praying it was Meredith saying it had all been a mistake, but it was his sister, Nan, calling to say hello. Philip mumbled that he didn't want to talk, but Nan finally forced him to explain what had happened. Against his protests, she said she'd be right over. When Nan finally appeared, she was carrying a pot of soup and an apple pie because she knew Philip hadn't finished his meal at the restaurant. Nan sat quietly with Philip while he toyed with his food, chatting about things her kids had done that day. After Philip grudgingly managed to eat a small amount of the meal, she put it away, gave him a hug, and agreed to leave only after Philip assured her that he would call if he needed her.

Philip took a bath to try and relax before going to sleep, but lying in bed the pain became overwhelming, and he couldn't stop thinking about what had happened. He thought about calling Meredith but phoned Nan instead, making sure that she had returned home safely and letting her know he was coping. Philip tried playing a tape of ocean waves to help his mind blank, but it only made him think about the aborted trip to Jamaica. He switched to some classical guitar music instead and eventually found himself drifting off to sleep.

By the time he got to work the next day, Philip was more in control of himself, but he still felt foggy and hurt. He told his friend Jim that he and Meredith had split up, and he'd had a rough night. Jim told Philip to go home, but when he said he would rather stay, Jim said that he would handle all the complex work orders and Philip could take the easier repairs. By the end of the day, Philip found that he was still suffering from the breakup, but he was not feeling as spacey or numb.

2

Hope

の

The initial shock has diminished. In its place is the knowledge, the realization that your lover has ended the relationship. It's over.

Or is it? After the shock phase, many people enter into a state of hope, feeling that if they just try hard enough, they can undo what has happened. If only they can be sufficiently clever or wonderful, then they can convince their lover to come back. In fact, this is one reason why the termination of a relationship can occasionally be more disruptive than the death of a loved one. When people pass away, their departure is final. When lovers leave, we can fantasize that the separation is not permanent.

The hope phase resembles the "protest" stage we saw in young children. When separated from their caregivers, they try anything—crying, screaming, running after them—to get them back. Adults in the hope stage engage in similar activities. They actively pursue their ex-lovers, calling them frequently on the telephone, sending them cards, going over to their house. They desperately try to negotiate with their lovers, promising to change themselves if only their lovers will come back to them. Vows to lose weight, stop nagging, and be more affectionate or less violent proliferate as a means of reestablishing a connection.

These attempts toward reconciliation can often reach extreme levels during this stage. One woman went to her ex-lover's house after he had left for work to iron his clothes, clean the place, and then prepare a dinner for when he returned. In another case, a man arranged to have breakfast delivered to his ex-lover's place of business every day, not just for her but for her entire office.

Frequently, this type of behavior can cause lovers to waiver in their decision, which of course increases the tendency for people to act this way to win them back. Unfortunately, the approach rarely works in the long run. After a period of temporary reconciliation, the problems that plagued the relationship in the first place usually recur, and often the termination is more painful the second time because the person not only feels rejected but also demeaned by his or her own groveling.

An even more serious pattern that can emerge during the hope stage is a form of emotional blackmail. Rejected partners will talk of becoming suicidal or self-injurious to elicit a compassionate response from their lovers. It takes an extremely unfeeling person to walk away from someone who threatens to hurt or kill herself. The lover returns to avoid serious consequences or more confrontation. Again, this rarely results in any permanent reconciliation. The lover is effectively held hostage, which destroys any chance of a normal relationship or the positive restoration of an emotional bond.

Consider what happened with Barbara, the physical therapist described in the shock section, whose lover said he was moving to Oregon, as she passed into the hope stage.

INTERVIEWER: What happened after the initial shock wore off?

BARBARA: A few days later, Nick and I were at his house. I had really gone overboard getting myself ready—I had my hair cut, my nails done, and bought something really sexy to wear. I guess I felt that if I was appealing enough, Nick wouldn't even consider leaving me. When I saw the boxes that he had been packing things up in, I just snapped. I started crying and screaming; I actually became so hysterical that I tore at my clothes and then started to claw at my face with my nails. Nick freaked out. He grabbed me and held me while telling me how sorry he was. He said that he loved me so much, he would never intentionally hurt me. Nick swore that he would stay in Maryland, and we would move in together, that things would be great. Eventually I calmed down and we sat together for a long time.

INTERVIEWER: So he stayed, and you two were together?

BARBARA: No. I felt like a real idiot the next day; I had trouble even believing how I had behaved. I told Nick that I was sorry, that I knew how much getting away from the East Coast meant to him, and that he meant so much to me that I couldn't ask him to stay. He begged me to consider coming with him, that he really did want me to be with him, and that his decision involved lifestyle and not love. I told him I would think about it. That we would call and write and visit with each other. We talked about when I would come out to Oregon to visit, so that I could see it and think about moving.

INTERVIEWER: How did that plan work out?

BARBARA: It didn't. Well, I guess it seemed all right for a while. I wrote Nick constantly and sent him newspaper clippings about local sports teams that he liked. I think I started out by writing every day, even twice a day. Nick never wrote, but we would talk three or four times a week, and he would make one or two of the calls. He was happy in Oregon, and he liked his job. After a month, I went out to visit. We had a great week and talked about my moving out there. Nick promised to try to find a job for me. I returned home and started making plans to leave, and even mentioned it to some of my friends, my family, and people I worked with.

But then Nick stopped calling me. He was cheerful enough when I phoned him, but he never initiated the calls. When I pressed him about whether he had any leads on jobs for me, he was very negative, telling me the economy was really down in the area and that positions were scarce, but he would keep looking. I received a professional journal in the mail about that time, and there were two positions listed close to where he lived. When I asked him about them, he said that they really weren't good jobs, that he didn't think I'd like the work.

INTERVIEWER: How did you feel about that?

BARBARA: It really confused me. I stopped calling for a week, just to see if Nick would call. He didn't. I panicked and called him, but I kept getting his machine. I called my travel agent and booked a flight out to Oregon the next weekend. I had to see him and work this out. A few days later, Nick answered the phone. He told me he had taken a short vacation, run down to California with a friend. I was stunned. He had told me that he would use any vacation time to be with me. When I confronted him with that, he passed it off, saying that it was just a short trip, that his friend had arranged it, and that it was no big deal. I told him that I planned to come out the following weekend, that I wanted to check out some of the jobs from the journal. Nick became very evasive and said that he was working all weekend, he wouldn't be able to see me, and it was a bad time.

INTERVIEWER: How did you react to that?

BARBARA: I was still feeling confused. I told Nick that maybe I should just move to Oregon and figure out the job situation once I was there. Nick became very cold. He said he had no intention of supporting me if I wasn't working. He also said that he was making a life for himself out there and didn't need anyone to watch over him. I was stunned. I told him not to worry, that I wouldn't keep bothering him, that I understood that he didn't want me anymore, and we were through. I think I expected him to correct me, to tell me how much he loved me, but he was just quiet. I said, "Good-bye, Nick," and hung up the phone.

INTERVIEWER: What happened then?

BARBARA: I became hysterical. I tried calling him back, but I kept getting a busy signal. He must have taken the phone off the hook, because I called all night. I finally got the operator to verify whether the line was working, and she said that the line was okay but that the phone was not hung up. When I called the next day, I got his answering machine and left a message for him to please call me, but he didn't. I was frantic. I considered using my ticket to fly out there or send him a bouquet of flowers to apologize. I couldn't think straight. It hurt so much, but I didn't know what to do about it.

Barbara tried to win Nick back, even after the signals were quite clear that he didn't want their relationship to continue. Often ex-lovers don't want to hurt you any more than they already have. When you pursue them, they hesitate or soften their words to avoid saying something cruel. You then perceive this as a weakening in their resolve to terminate the relationship. Your hope renews, and your efforts to get them back intensify until they finally say something mean enough to get you to stop.

So what do you do? The biologically programmed drive to get someone back is exacerbated by adult ingenuity and willfulness. Unfortunately, the pursuit and manipulation isn't productive in the long run, so you don't get what you set out to obtain, or, if you do, and your lover comes back to you, it is typically under duress.

Strategies for the Hope Stage

Again, it is important to realize that most people go through this stage. You're not likely to avoid it. But you can do things to make your passage through the phase more bearable and to ensure that you won't get stuck. This is crucial because the hope stage can be a self-perpetuating cycle—you try to get your lover back, he or she waivers, you try harder, he or she relents, the two of you get back together, your lover leaves, and the whole thing starts all over. To avoid this painful and repetitive process you need to focus on actions that are productive and protective and consider your own needs rather than your ex-lover's.

The overall goal for the hope stage should be to:

✧

**Change the Focus
from Accommodating Your Lover
to Pleasing Yourself!!**

✧

This isn't always easy, but it is possible, and it feels a lot better than demeaning yourself.

DELAY YOUR ACTIONS.

If you plan to call or write your lover, make yourself wait a specified period of time before you do. A cooling-off interval may help you decide that you really don't want to follow through with what you had planned.

Enlist a friend's help. Make it a rule that any contact with your lover has to be preceded by contacting your friend. Before you call your lover, make sure that you call your friend first. If you want to write to your lover, you need to write to your friend first. The same thing goes for visits, presents, and good deeds. Whatever you wish to do for your lover needs to be done for your friend first. Of course it's possible that with all this attention your friend might be sorry once you get past this stage!

CHANNEL YOUR IMPULSES.

If you feel the desire to do something nice for your ex-lover, try directing the impulse toward someone who needs or deserves it.

- Before you give your ex-lover a gift, bring one to a nursing home or shelter.
- Do you feel the need to write a letter to your lover? Volunteer instead to help with a letter-writing campaign or a mailing for a charity that appeals to you.

Not only will you feel helpful, you'll be around people who actually appreciate your effort.
- Do you have the impulse to cook or clean for your ex-lover? Why not make a meal for an elderly relative or teach a younger one how to create culinary masterpieces.

In short, it's better to help those who will appreciate your work and cherish you for your effort.

DECIDE WHAT YOU REALLY WANT TO CHANGE.

It should be obvious that you can't undo events that have already happened, but that usually doesn't stop people from tormenting themselves about things anyway. You repeat scenes from the past in your head, running over and over them, wishing you had said this or done that. But that doesn't change what *did* happen, and in reality, a different response from you probably wouldn't have altered things.

Since you can't affect what has already happened, it's better to concentrate on aspects of your personality or behavior patterns that you might wish to change for the future. Don't pick on yourself or put yourself down, just choose some small improvements that will make life and loving better for you.

Make sure that the aspects you target for improvement are parts of you that *you* wish to change, not just things that you would alter to please your ex-lover. If you want to lose weight or stop smoking, fine, if this is important to *you* and not a reaction to something your lover once said. Your lover's judgment is suspect anyway, since he or she didn't have the good sense to stay with you!

Make a list with two columns. Mark one with the heading "Things I want to change about myself" and the other with the heading "Things my lover would want me to change." Find one thing that is on your list but not on your lover's. Choose this as a target for self-improvement. You'll use up some of that energy you want to direct toward pleasing your lover, but in a way that actually achieves your own goals.

When you work toward improving yourself, realize that the benefits will be for you in the future—you won't change what's already happened or bring your lover back. Be content in knowing that an "improved" you is a positive result of the ending of your relationship, a gift that will really pay off in the years ahead.

Remember—make sure the changes you choose are small, attainable, and important to *you*, not your lover.

GET IN TOUCH WITH THE "OLD" YOU.

Being in a relationship often means that we forgo some of the things we like to do in order to spend time with our lover. Now that the relationship is over, you can reconnect with your old life.

Make a list of activities that you used to enjoy before you started this relationship, things you just haven't had the time or energy to do since you met your lover. Before the relationship, did you play the piano, go canoeing, attend the symphony? Have you given up reading mystery novels, working with the recycling center, or painting? Make an effort to reinvolve yourself in the activities that you used to love before your lover took their place.

The same holds true for people. Contact friends you haven't seen in a while, especially ones that seemed to go by the wayside once you found your lover. Reestablish connections with any group activities (line dancing, softball, chess clubs) that you gave up when you became part of a couple.

TAKE AN INVENTORY OF YOUR LOVER'S GOOD AND BAD POINTS.

Make a list of your lover's good and bad points. Start by examining positive traits. What is it that you really miss about him or her? Is it your lover's sense of humor or stimulating conversation? For each of your lover's good points, try to think of how you could find this characteristic in another person or activity. Can you compensate for those qualities by doing something else? Can someone or something else make you laugh, feel less lonely, or feel appreciated? One man said that he missed the conversations he had with his lover after work, that they allowed him to defuse his day. He found similar results by joining a racquetball club and whacking a ball around after work, talking to people at the club instead of going right home to an empty house.

Now take a look at your lover's bad points. Ask yourself why you still want to pursue someone who was everything you just wrote down. Do you really want to be involved with someone who is cold, who lies, who is stubborn? Consider whether you miss a romanticized image of your lover or the real person. Make sure that you don't idealize or glamorize the person who has left. Pull out that list of bad points whenever you find yourself doing this and take a good look at it.

Often when you make a list of all the good and bad points your lover had, you realize that the loss you feel is not for the person but for the relationship itself, or, very often, what you *wanted* it to be. Pursuing your lover will only bring back the old reality; your ideal lies in the future with someone else.

AFFIRM THAT THE RELATIONSHIP IS OVER.

It's important to verbalize that the relationship has ended, even if you don't really believe it or you don't want it to be true. By speaking it out loud, it may help you resolve things faster, because you'll be dealing with the reality of the termination instead of the possibilities inside your head. Verbalizing that you and your lover are no longer together gives you the power and commitment to deal with that fact.

So, several times a day, make a positive statement that your relationship with your lover is over. Make sure that you say it *out loud.*

Make definite statements to your friends and family about your breakup. You'd be surprised at the number of people who don't say anything even to the people closest to them, clinging to the hope that things will resolve, that the separation won't be permanent. Making a positive declaration that your relationship has ended will make you feel clearer and more settled and will also enable others to give you much needed support.

DECIDE HOW FAR YOU ARE WILLING TO GO.

If you're determined to pursue your lover, ask yourself how far you will go in order to please him or her. What act would you perceive as being too demeaning, too manipulative? How does that behavior differ from how you have been acting so far?

Sometimes by exaggerating an action, it helps us see our behavior in a new light and makes it more difficult to rationalize our actions. So if you were planning to send your lover a card, make sure it is the most expensive, elaborate card you can find. Why not have it hand delivered by a messenger along with balloons and a song? Have the envelope addressed by a calligrapher. Ridiculous? So might be sending the card. By forcing yourself to adopt extreme behavior, you may decide that the original idea wasn't very good either!

WRITE YOURSELF A STORY.

Try to remember a time when your lover was particularly horrible to you, a time he or she might have been extremely mean or vicious, or treated you worse than anyone else ever had. Write the event out as a story—a "once upon a time" sort of thing. Make it as explicit and detailed as possible. For example—

> Once upon a time there was a man named Bob. Bob used to take his girlfriend Kathy with him when he went to company dinners. When everyone was quiet, Bob would point out that Kathy had spilled food on her dress, or was chewing with her mouth open, or had said something stupid. He made sure that everyone looked at her and laughed. He would usually keep this up until Kathy left the table in tears, and then he'd say, "There she goes again, always so melodramatic."

The next time you are tempted to do something nice for your ex-lover, read the story first. See if what you are about to do would be a logical conclusion to the tale.

FIGURE OUT WHAT IS DISTRESSING YOU.

Clarify within yourself why you are upset. Was your lover really the right person for you or were you just comfortable together? Do you genuinely want your lover back, or are you embarrassed, lonely, or afraid?

One woman pursued her lover even though he was an alcoholic who occasionally beat her when he got drunk. She finally realized that she didn't want him, she was just afraid she would never find anyone else, and she was afraid of being alone. Another man was furious at the thought that the woman who dumped him thought she was better than he was. He tried to win her back with the hope of punishing her and proving his superiority.

Whatever the case, be clear about your real issues so that you can deal with them. Are you afraid of being alone, hurt at being abandoned, embarrassed by someone you felt was actually your inferior, or humiliated in front of family or friends? Once you have pinpointed the problem, you can take steps to resolve it in ways other than re-instituting the relationship.

Passing Through the Hope Stage

Margaret, a twenty-seven-year-old representative for a software company, had a particularly difficult time in the hope stage but worked her way out of it. Margaret met George six months after her divorce. George was every-thing her husband had not been—mature, settled, and supportive of Margaret as a person. She hadn't planned on getting attached so soon, but their first dates were so won-derful that there seemed to be an almost magical connec-tion between them.

George moved into Margaret's house, and at first, every-thing seemed to be going great. They talked about getting married, rarely fought, and had an exciting intimate rela-tionship. Then George's behavior began to change. He would tell Margaret how much he wanted to get married and then would say that he had doubts about their rela-tionship. Sometimes he would beg her to accompany him when he went away, and then he would scream at her for not giving him any space. One day George rang up and said that he was not coming back from his business trip, that the relationship was over. During the next few days when she didn't hear from him, Margaret experienced the reactions of the shock stage.

INTERVIEWER: How did you get out of it?

MARGARET: George called to tell me he was at his sister's and that he was sorry. He loved me so much and knew that he had not been rational lately. We'd work it all out.

INTERVIEWER: And did you?

MARGARET: No. He kept going back and forth like that. I would get really upset when he pulled away from me, and he would start placating me. I was so confused I couldn't tell if I was in a relationship or not. I cried all the time, and then George would call and tell me how much he loved me. I dropped everything to be with him. I'd stop what I was doing just to bring him his favorite cookies. One time I helped him get out a report, even when my own work was lagging behind. I changed my whole schedule around just to be there when he wanted me to, or I sat home just in case he called.

INTERVIEWER: How did you resolve this?

MARGARET: I finally realized that I couldn't control George; I could only control myself. I started taking care of myself better, doing my work, indulging myself. I stopped planning my day around George and did things that I wanted to do. I don't think I had read a book the whole time we were together, and it was something that I used to do a lot. I went to the library and got a whole stack of books. I picked one up whenever I got the urge to run over to see George and forced myself to read at least fifty pages first.

INTERVIEWER: What happened when George approached you?

MARGARET: I was happy to talk to him if he called, but I stuck to my own schedule. If he wanted to fit into it, then fine. The funny thing is that my independence made George more attentive at first, but he was still wildly ambivalent in his behavior. I began to notice that I was happier when I wasn't in contact with him. I also came to realize that all that ambivalence was actually his way of trying to end things; he just didn't have the courage to come right out and do it. When I kept doing things to please him, it made him even weaker. I finally knew that it was time to let go, so the next time he said he felt insecure about us, I agreed and suggested ending things.

INTERVIEWER: How did you feel when it was totally over?

MARGARET: I had moments when I missed him a lot. I was also furious at myself for how I had groveled to get him back. I took control of things at the end, though. I acted strongly and that felt pretty good.

In this case, Margaret's pursuit of George made his natural ambivalent tendencies even stronger and prolonged the eventual termination of their relationship. It was only when she took steps to focus on her own needs that the situation became resolved.

If you still feel the need to pursue your ex-lover, consider this interview with Martin, a habitual leaver, and his insights concerning the actions of women with whom he has terminated relationships.

INTERVIEWER: What would make you want to end a relationship?

MARTIN: Boredom. Or if she drove me crazy by being too demanding. Sometimes I'd seen somebody better.

INTERVIEWER: How did you usually end a relationship with a woman? Were you direct or did you use more indirect approaches?

MARTIN: Usually I was more indirect about it. I would begin to taper off my involvement with the woman by not phoning her as much, not taking her out as often.

INTERVIEWER: Why didn't you end the relationship right away?

MARTIN: Because I wanted to avoid confrontation, and I didn't want to hurt her feelings.

INTERVIEWER: Didn't you eventually have to deal with the confrontation?

MARTIN: Yes, but the ending of the relationship usually came from the woman instead of me.

INTERVIEWER: You provoked her into breaking up with you?

MARTIN: Yes, by being passive and disinterested. It forced her to question the relationship. Once she brought up the status of our relationship, once it was on the table, it was easier to end it.

INTERVIEWER: Were you ever direct in ending a relationship?

MARTIN: I can remember two times when I was direct. I wanted to be more grown-up and take responsibility for the termination of the relationship, instead of taking a more passive, manipulative role.

INTERVIEWER: After breaking up with a woman, was there anything she could do that would change your mind about ending the relationship?

MARTIN: Yes. If she talked about changing her behavior, I might try again. I guess I felt some pressure to try. But it never really changed things in the long run, and the relationship never worked out. It really just delayed the inevitable.

INTERVIEWER: Do you have any advice for women, or for people in general, about terminating relationships?

MARTIN: I guess I'd just say to let go and be done with it. I mean, why would they want someone back who didn't want to be there? I never could understand what women thought they had gained if they managed to drag me back, just to have us break up again later. After seeing a woman grovel, I never could have respect for her again. What really impressed me were those women who had enough style to just get mad and then let go, who realized that it was over and got on with their lives.

3

Anger

Once you recover from the initial shock and have seen that pleading and negotiating for your lover's return produces no long-term solution, you become angry. This stage can be frightening since actions often take an aggressive or destructive form. You feel furious about how you were treated. You become irate when you remember how selfish your lover has been, even with all the love that you gave. Your lover has turned your life upside down, bashed your ego, and you feel it's time to express how angry you are about it. Gone are thoughts of continuing the relationship; you just want to hurt your lover the way you were hurt. You mentally calculate ways of making him or her suffer. You vent your anger to your friends and to those who you feel could harm your lover the most. Your goal becomes revenge.

Obviously this stage is most serious when the anger

gets out of control. Rather than freeing you from your old relationship, your rage binds you to your lover in a web of retaliation. Instead of being a positive release of emotion directed toward an appropriate source, your anger develops a life of its own.

Barbara's hope of restoring her relationship with Nick and moving to Oregon changed into a dangerous, angry vengeance.

INTERVIEWER: Did you continue pursuing Nick even after he avoided you?

BARBARA: Well, one day I came home and there was finally a message on my machine from Nick. I was really excited until I heard what he had to say. He told me never to bother him again, that if I kept calling he would file charges for harassment. I went berserk. All of this rage came pouring out of me. I called him up and when I got his machine, I left this hate message. I told him that he was so disgusting that I was going to call the physical therapy board in his state and tell them that he had once been a cocaine user. When I hung up, I was still furious. I remember running out of my house, screaming, until I was way up the street. After a while I calmed down and went back home. Nick called that night. He was full of apologies, said that he had been stressed out over work, and that he hadn't meant to leave such a cold message. But I was beyond falling for all of that. I remember shouting at him that he was a spineless wimp, that he had run away rather than deal with our relationship back in Maryland. He screamed back at me that I was unstable, and that after the night when I had hurt myself, he had been afraid to tell me it was over because I might kill myself. Then he said that if I told anyone about his past cocaine use he would tell them that I was a stalker, and he had the phone records to prove it. I slammed down the phone.

Barbara perceived her behavior as justified because of what Nick had done to her. Her actions became so intense, however, that they were distressing rather than helping her.

Strategies for the Anger Stage

Anger works best as a release, a venting of emotion. When it gets tied to action and used to harm someone, the negativity can distort your perceptions and warp your judgment. The goals for getting through the anger phase successfully and healthfully are:

✑

Vent Your Feelings.

Transform Your Anger into Creative, Constructive Actions.

✑

VENT YOUR ANGER.

You need to release your feelings so that they don't overwhelm you. Anger is a volatile emotion, one that creates a need to move, to act. You can channel this impulse in nonaggressive ways:

- Vent to a friend. Find someone who is willing to listen to you scream, rant, rave, and threaten. If it helps, imagine that your friend is your ex-lover while you do it.
- Yell at a tree. Kick it if you want. The leaves will absorb your words, and your kicks probably won't make a dent.
- Punch and strangle your pillows. Softer on the body than trees, pillows can take quite a lot of active punishment.

FIND A POSITIVE OUTLET FOR YOUR ANGER.

As mentioned earlier, anger creates movement, a desire to act. Why not direct all of that energy in a positive way? Any vigorous activity will do; the more energy you expend the better. It helps even more to select a task that will benefit you in some way. For instance:

- Scrubbing your floors is a strenuous activity with a gratifying result. It is also a great metaphor for cleaning up the problem.

- Physical exercise is beneficial at this point. Within your own limitations, choose an activity that is as energetic as possible, such as kickboxing or aerobics, and do it until you are fairly exhausted. It allows you to release your aggression and conditions your body at the same time.

The action you choose is not critical. The important thing is to act, move, exert. Thinking won't discharge all of that pent-up anger—you need to release it in a more physical way. It's also very hard to be angry when your body is exhausted!

RETURN YOUR LOVER'S BELONGINGS OR GIFTS BY MAIL OR HAVE A FRIEND DELIVER THEM.

It's important to cleanse the space around you and get rid of all of the connections that incite you, assuming that you are past the hope stage and are not using the return of the belongings as a ploy to see your lover and entice him or her back to you. At this point, it's usually better to use an intermediary so that contact with your ex-partner doesn't turn into a shouting match or worse. Do this to purge your old relationship; don't make it into a scene that will tie you to your ex-lover.

WRITE A LETTER ABOUT YOUR ANGER.

Sometimes it helps to write a letter to your lover expressing how angry you are about what happened. However, it's a good idea to mail it to yourself first. After you receive it, and read it over, you can decide whether you want to actually send it. If you decide to mail it to your lover, make sure the letter expresses your anger but is not threatening in any way. This will ensure that you avoid any legal or emotional ramifications.

APPLY YOURSELF AT WORK.

During the shock phase, you probably let your work slide. During the hope stage, you focused all of your attention on how to get your lover back. Why not take all of your anger and channel it into excelling at work? If you really feel the need to take revenge on your lover, why not do it by being energetic and creative at your job? This will help redirect your anger and also give you some positive strokes. What could be better vindication than being outstanding at what you do?

USE RITUALS FOR THEIR EXTREMELY POWERFUL AND CLEANSING PROPERTIES.

It's not surprising that most of the world's religions and cultures make use of rituals, acts that are conducted with great solemnity and ceremony. By investing a simple thing with formality and seriousness, you can make it powerful. Rituals can provide a deeper sense of closure and enable you to release your anger. Here are some examples that might work as panaceas:

- Make a pile of your lover's pictures or love letters. Tear them into small pieces and place them in a fireproof container. As you burn the paper, visualize your relationship with your lover ending and the smoke purifying your body.
- Conduct a funeral for your relationship. Place mementos, pictures, and letters in a small box and dig a hole to bury them. Invite friends over for the ceremony if you like. Say a few words at the "grave site," and then fill in the hole, burying the past.
- Find a plant or tree that needs pruning. With each snip, visualize that you are cutting your ties to your lover. Verbalize that fact with every clip, actually saying something like "With this snip, I am cutting my ties to [lover's name]."

Passing Through the Anger Stage

Carol, a freshman in college, reacted in anger when her relationship with her boyfriend, Walter, terminated. The pair had known each other since childhood. Carol was literally the girl next door, but they had never been close friends because Walter was three years older. Romance started when they met at a fraternity party at the beginning of Carol's freshman year. They had been seeing each other exclusively for close to six months.

INTERVIEWER: How did things fall apart?
CAROL: I had a late class on Thursday nights. I would

usually go to see Walter at his frat house afterwards. My class had been canceled because of a death in my professor's family, so I went straight over to Walter's room. When I got there his door was closed but I could hear voices coming from inside. I figured he was watching TV so I threw open the door, singing, "Honey, I'm home," to be funny. Only it wasn't so funny, because Walter was in bed with someone else. I'd seen her around, but I didn't know her name. I screamed, I think, and then ran out.

INTERVIEWER: What happened after that?

CAROL: Walter came by to explain, but I wasn't in the mood to listen. I heard what he was saying, but he had lost total credibility with me. I couldn't believe a word he had to say. I told him to shut up and go away, to leave me alone. He started by saying how much he loved me, but then he got really ugly. He told me that he needed to be with other women because I was lousy in bed. He told me he had never planned on being faithful to me, even after we got married. He figured that it was probably better that things ended this way, before we got even more involved. Then he walked out.

INTERVIEWER: What did you do?

CAROL: I'm not really proud of my behavior looking back. It's just that I was so angry, really pissed at him. Several days after our breakup, I went to the parking lot where he kept his car and used my key to scratch the word "asshole" in the paint. I sent him some dead flowers. One day when I knew he wasn't going to be in his room, I snuck in there and cut all the buttons off of every piece of clothing he owned.

INTERVIEWER: Did any of that help you get over him?

CAROL: Actually, I think it made me feel good for a little while, like this temporary high. I'd get really pumped up when I was planning things and after I did them. But it really didn't make me feel better in the long run. And I got really obsessed with trying to think of things to do to him. It felt pretty unhealthy.

INTERVIEWER: How did you stop?

CAROL: Things sort of got worse. I went home for a visit and told my parents what had happened, only I told them that the person in bed had been a guy. They had known Walter and his family for a long time. I knew my mother couldn't keep things to herself and that she would spread this through the neighborhood. Eventually it got back to Walter's mother, and she and my mom had a real screaming match. It was horrible. But it broke me down. I started crying. My mother got very upset with me for using her to spread malicious rumors, which made me feel even worse. I think it shook me back to my senses enough to realize I had to stop doing all those things.

INTERVIEWER: How did you regain control?

CAROL: Well, first I apologized to my mother. I explained that I had really messed up, but I was sorry about it and wanted to make it up to her. She had me write an apology to Walter's family for spreading rumors about him, and together we took it over to his parents' house along with a cake. It was a fairly horrible experience because of how angry and hurt they were, but I felt better that I had at least faced up to the consequences of my actions. I threw myself into my schoolwork, which helped to take my mind off of what I had done. I still got pretty mad whenever I would see Walter at school, but I yelled about it to my friends instead of doing something destructive. My friend Ellie convinced me to attend her karate classes with her. I really enjoyed all the kicking and punching, and it helped me act out how I was feeling in a safe way. I also think the instructor's attitudes toward nonviolence helped me control myself as well.

INTERVIEWER: How do you feel about things now?

CAROL: I'm really ashamed of what I did, but it felt good that I could finally act more rationally.

4

Despair

⚖

When the anger fades, many individuals turn their feelings inward. Concerns regarding the role you played in the breakup of your relationship filter into your thoughts. You begin to have misgivings about yourself. Inside your head you continuously play tapes, going over the time you were with your lover, agonizing over what you could have or should have done differently. You question your past actions or your inability to see any warning signs. You are tormented by your shortcomings. At the very least you question your ability to judge people correctly. You start to think that maybe you didn't know him or her at all. Why didn't you see your lover for what he or she was? Why weren't you able to see what was coming?

Often you feel unlovable or unworthy. Perhaps your lover was correct in the decision to leave you. Maybe no one will ever find you desirable again. Gradually you become more depressed. Everything begins to lose its appeal. Going out with friends is a chore. You'd rather stay home and watch television or sleep.

Despair is actually similar to shock, but on a psychological rather than a physiological level. In shock, the body closes down all unnecessary functioning; in despair, you close yourself off from the outside world, shutting out any intrusions. In the initial shock stage, however, your mind often feels numb and hazy; in despair, it won't shut down. Ruminations run rampant; you often can't get your thoughts to slow down or stop. It seems the more you wall yourself off from the world, the more active your mind becomes.

After Barbara's rage at Nick had subsided, she entered a period of doubting herself.

INTERVIEWER: How long did you stay angry with Nick?

BARBARA: For a while. I was furious at how he had misled me, how he had strung me along. I mean, I could have left my job and moved, all for someone who didn't care about me. After a while, the things he said really started to hurt. I think that the things I had done upset me almost as much. I became depressed. I started to hate myself. No wonder Nick hadn't loved me. I was an unstable, unworthy piece of shit. I felt horrible. I picked my appearance apart every time I looked in the mirror. My work really started to go downhill.

INTERVIEWER: Did anything help?

BARBARA: At the time I was really resistant to anyone's

help. I stopped seeing all my friends, I pulled back from my family. I didn't go anywhere except work, and half the time I didn't get there on time. When someone criticized my job performance, I didn't care. I knew I was a mess, but what did they expect? Nick had been right. I was unstable, I couldn't do anything right, why should I even try?

Barbara's despair resulted in her pulling away from her friends and life. Unfortunately, the more self-absorbed she became, the less healing could occur. It is important to keep self-deprecation within limits. There are plenty of people out there who are willing to put you down—you just ended a relationship with one of them—don't add yourself to the list!

Strategies for the Despair Stage

No matter how badly you feel, it's important to try to get through this stage as quickly as possible. Despair can be a trap, a bog, pulling you down and keeping you there. Hope, anger, and despair are the most common stages in which to become stuck. Despair can sometimes be the hardest to move out of since you generally feel immobilized, and you pull away from people who could give you reasonable feedback or extra help. There are a number of effective strategies, however, that can be used at this stage to stop the despair and get on with your healing. Your major goals at this time should be:

❧

Drop the Past in Order to Focus on the Future.

Let Go of Blame and Reach for Solutions.

❧

KEEP IN TOUCH.

When you're feeling down, it's easy to pull away from everyone, but now is not a good time for isolation.

- Make a list of those people who have been supportive and helpful to you so far. Try to call one of them every day so that you feel appreciated and not isolated.
- Make another list of the people you know who are the most fun. Try to spend as much time with them as possible. Laughter might seem impossible, but it's worth a try.
- Place yourself in group activities. Sign up for that class you always wanted to take, get involved in a local political issue, join a fund-raising drive or a bowling team. Even if you don't want to go out or see people, it will help you to make the effort.

TUNE INTO THE BIGGER PICTURE.

When we are having problems, they tend to fill our whole lives. It helps to scale them down by getting a broader perspective.

- Take a walk in the mountains, by the ocean, or under a sky of stars. Our problems tend to diminish in the presence of energies so much older and larger in scale than ourselves.
- Volunteer to do charity work. Besides getting you out of the house and into contact with people, it will connect you with others who are also needy.
- Expand the spiritual side of your life. Seek out religious or mystical experiences. Go to a Bible study class, learn to read Tarot cards, attend a Zen meditation session. Get out of your head and into your spirit for a while.

STIR THE SOUP.

If you leave a pot of soup alone for a while, all the solid bits fall to the bottom and the fat rises to the top. To keep things even and prevent settling, you have to give it a stir. The same thing happens to us when we become withdrawn and sedentary—the parts start to settle, and our minds get clogged. You need to act if you want to get things functioning in a more healthful way.

Exercise your mind in a productive manner. Read a book, take a course, go to a lecture, or learn a foreign language. Try to get your thoughts working for you instead of keeping them fixated on your past relationship. If you're going to be mentally exhausted, it might as well be from something that will benefit you in the future.

Exercise your body. You may not need the vigorous activity required in the anger stage, but it would probably help you feel better if you can just get moving. Take a walk or a bicycle ride. Start a new routine, like an early morning run. If you're finding it hard to get started, convince yourself to spend just five minutes a day in the activity. Then you can gradually extend the amount of time invested. You'll find that the effort required to get moving is less each day, and you might actually look forward to it.

PAMPER YOURSELF.

You've been through an ordeal, and you deserve to be nurtured and spoiled. Now is not the time to be stingy with yourself. While it is sometimes difficult to indulge yourself in pleasurable activities when you are feeling low, this is exactly what you need to do. It will not only change your mood but will help make you feel more attractive and deserving.

Treat yourself to a facial, a massage, a haircut, some new clothes. Go to a special cafe with a friend and order a dessert that you've always resisted because it was too expensive or high in calories. Watch a video that you've always wanted to see. Wear an outfit that makes you feel attractive or sophisticated.

Think back to times when you have indulged yourself or done things that made you really happy. Now is the time to call in those sensations and re-create them as often as possible.

REWRITE THE TAPES PLAYING INSIDE YOUR HEAD.

If you find yourself unable to stop thinking about what happened and continually play scenes inside your head, at least rewrite them in a positive way. Give up the "if only's" and the "shoulds." Take the scene and rescript it, as if you were writing a new movie plot. Write it down so that you and your lover behave exactly how you wish you would have. Now look at the differences between the script you just wrote and how you actually acted in reality. This will give you a better idea about areas that you need to improve for future relationships. In your script, did you listen more? Did you nag less? Did you stand up for yourself better? Now look at the differences in your lover's behavior in the script and in reality. Was your lover more romantic? More compassionate? Less critical? The differences will give you a good idea of what to search for in a future partner.

SCHEDULE YOUR DOWNTIMES.

It is helpful to focus the despair you feel rather than have it permeate your entire day. Choose a time when you can ritualize your sadness and make an appointment with your feelings. Set a beginning and end point—for instance, schedule to have despair from 7:15 to 7:45 every morning. Never make the planned time last longer than half an hour or you will become too depressed. Use a clock or timer to regulate the session.

During your scheduled "sad time," allow yourself to think about what is bothering you. Play music that fits your mood and surround yourself with objects that make you feel low, such as a picture of your ex-lover.

When the time is up, you have to put all negative thoughts and objects away until the next scheduled despair session. If you find yourself crying or feeling low at any other point, remind yourself that you are free to act that way or think those thoughts, but only during the appropriate time of day.

During the despair session, make sure that you feel safe. If you don't feel strong enough to handle all of those negative thoughts and emotions, shorten the length of the appointed time. Or, you might want to have a friend or family member present when you do the ritual.

By scheduling and confronting your sadness directly, you will begin to gain control over your feelings and loosen their effects on your life. You will gradually be able to shorten the amount of time you spend in despair and limit the impact it has on other parts of your day.

LOOK FOR THE POSITIVES.

When you are feeling bad, it seems like despair fills every part of your day. But there are often some times during the day or night when you don't feel quite as bad. Try and investigate why that might be. What were you doing at that point? Who were you with? It may be that if you spent

more time doing those activities or surrounded yourself
with those positive people, you might actually spend less
time feeling sad.

See the positives in yourself as well. Make a list of your
assets and strengths rather than your weaknesses. How
can you use these to make your life even better? If you see
being honest as one of your positive traits, you might want
to do some service work for a consumer group. Compassionate? Perhaps you could work helping others. Creative?
Start a new art project or write a song. Loving? Adopt a
puppy or kitten from the SPCA. Whatever your strengths,
you can use them to open up possibilities. Applaud your
virtues and accept them as a real part of making you a person who should be valued.

Passing Through the Despair Stage

Lorena, a twenty-four-year-old nurse, was filled with
doubts about her self-worth after a traumatic breakup
with Tony. She spent her time sitting at home watching
television and crying. Lorena even began to miss work because she couldn't bring herself to face people.

INTERVIEWER: What finally pulled you out of your de-
    pression?
LORENA: I wallowed in my misery for quite a while, not
    allowing anyone to interrupt my self-loathing. Fi-
    nally, a group of my friends "kidnapped" me. They
    picked me up from my house and threw me in the
    car. They dragged me out to this crafts festival in

Harpers Ferry. I was furious at the time and acted really sullen. But I think the feeling that somebody cared about me penetrated somehow. By the end of the day, I was feeling better and knew that I had to do something to get over my breakup with Tony. By the time we got back to my house, I invited everyone in, and we all got silly making ridiculous toasts to each other.

INTERVIEWER: What else seemed to work?

LORENA: I think once I let my friends back in, I started to be able to do some other things to distract myself. There was a call at work for people interested in providing some help for children of homeless families who were falling in between the cracks of normal services. I volunteered my time, and I found that I rarely thought about my own issues when I was working there. I liked the people contact, and it filled up some of the empty space and time. It also made me feel ashamed to be so dramatic about my problems when faced with some real crisis situations. Everyone was so grateful for my help that it made me start to feel better about my own worth, and how I fit into the big picture. I think it made me much more responsible at my own job because I started thinking of myself as "Lorena, the competent helper" as opposed to "Lorena, the loser."

5

Indifference

❧

The pain, anger, and despair eventually diminish, and you begin to feel more in control. You're surprised as thoughts of your lover come infrequently, and those thoughts you do have are not really emotionally charged or painful. You have no need to seek out your lover, and you don't worry about whether you are going to bump into him or her.

You can now put the relationship into better perspective, viewing it either as an experience you don't wish to duplicate or one that helped you to grow as a person. You are ready to establish your identity as an independent person, one who is no longer attached or reactive to your ex-lover.

One of the great challenges of this stage is to develop an understanding that alone does not necessarily mean lonely. Within our society there are often pressures to date and mate, so that single individuals are sometimes thought to be deviant or inadequate in some way.

It helps to view being single as being independent. Try to enjoy your time by yourself. After all, you can do what you want, when you want to do it, which is a luxury for most people in relationships. Relish your freedom, enjoy your solitude, and know that by developing yourself as a strong, separate human being, you are taking the first step toward promoting positive future relationships. As you become aware that you have the strength and ability to satisfy your own needs, future relationships will be based on choice rather than necessity.

As she enters into the indifference stage, Barbara seems very different from the emotional woman we have seen previously.

INTERVIEWER: How have things changed for you?

BARBARA: For a long time if I thought about Nick, I would become angry or start to cry. Sometimes I would have this sort of empty longing, I missed him so much. It was so ridiculous that even the word "Oregon" would throw me into a funk, and when I heard certain songs that we both liked, or saw one of his friends, I would fall apart. Six months after we split up, I went to a national therapy conference, and the thought that Nick might be there threw me into an emotional frenzy. Part of me feared seeing him, part of me wanted to bump into him. I was so strung out. I checked the registration table three times a day to see if he had come. I don't know if I was relieved or disappointed that he didn't show up.

INTERVIEWER: But you don't feel that way now?

BARBARA: It's kind of amazing. I'm not sure when things even began to change, whether it happened gradually or all at once. I would see something that reminded me of Nick and expect the emotional reaction, but it just didn't come. I could go, "Yeah, we liked to eat there on Sundays," when someone mentioned a particular restaurant, but the pain wasn't there anymore.

INTERVIEWER: Have you started seeing anyone else?

BARBARA: I'm not sure I'm quite ready for that. I feel comfortable going out with friends right now, and I don't really have a problem talking to people. And I'm beginning to like myself a lot better. I just don't know if I feel quite ready to jump into another relationship.

Strategies for the Indifference Stage

Indifference marks the first step toward freeing yourself from your past relationship. Your goals during this phase should be:

∂

Develop and Enjoy Your Independence.

Build the Foundation for Future Relationships.

∂

Make a list of the ways you've changed.

You've undergone quite a few changes since your lover left you. Make a list of all the ways you feel like you're different from the person you used to be. You might be calmer now, more creative, or more willing to speak your mind.

Go through the list and check those changes that you feel are positive, those new facets that you think you should hang on to or develop. You might want to continue being opinionated but prefer not to be as driven at work.

Place an *X* next to those changes that were useful, that helped protect and heal you but are no longer necessary. For instance, you might have become either very flirtatious or icy cold since the breakup, but those behaviors don't seem to suit you right now.

We can shape who we want to be. Look at all the traits that you have checked and decide what you need to do to ensure they continue. Examine any characteristics you might have placed an *X* next to and think about how to do them less often.

Plan for a new lover.

Given that we often get what we wish for, be as clear and specific as possible about what you hope to find in a new relationship. Make a list of all the qualities that you would like to have in a new lover, and another list of all the traits you would like him or her definitely *not* to have.

If you're having difficulty coming up with ideas, think

of those people in your life who make you feel good or whom you respect. Just what is it about them that makes you feel that way? Is it their appearance, their sense of humor, their ambition, their compassion? Have you realized you can't stand people who smoke, lie, or bite their nails? Be clear about what you'd like to find in your next lover and what you definitely want to avoid.

DECIDE WHAT KIND OF RELATIONSHIP YOU WISH TO HAVE WITH YOUR FORMER LOVER.

Now that you are able to think clearly and nonemotionally, you might want to decide what kind of relationship, if any, you wish to have with your ex-lover. Do you want him or her as a friend, a fading memory, or someone with whom you have no contact at all? Your decision will be based on many factors, including how the relationship ended, how you feel about your ex-lover as a person, and your own needs.

Some people feel comfortable having an ex-lover as a friend, others wouldn't even consider the possibility. Isn't it nice to know, though, that you can sit back and make the decision with no emotional pain at all?

SET NEW GOALS FOR YOURSELF PERSONALLY AND PROFESSIONALLY.

You're feeling stronger. You're independent. What do you want to do with your life? Take some time to evaluate your personal and career goals.

What does the "new" you want to accomplish? Are you growing or stagnating? Are you unsure of the direction you want to take next? You're blessed with time and space to think now—why not use it to take stock of exactly what you want to do with the rest of your life? You may find you're happy with who and where you are, or you might decide to embark on an adventure or a new career. What a great opportunity!

SPEND TIME WITH ALL SORTS OF PEOPLE OF DIFFERENT AGES.

So often in our lives we get stuck interacting with the same people, people who are a lot like us. Why not use some of your free time to socialize with people who differ from you, people from different cultural backgrounds, people of different ages? Be a Scout troop leader, coach a Little League team, deliver meals on wheels to the elderly, or teach music at a nursing home.

Learn to value what is special about each new person and to sense when you have concerns as well. Write a list if it helps to clarify your reactions. This is not only a great way to gain experience but also to learn to trust your emotional judgment again.

VISUALIZE YOURSELF AS A POWERFUL, BALANCED HUMAN BEING.

Find a quiet space and settle into a comfortable position. Close your eyes and relax your breathing. Now get a picture inside your head of yourself as happy and in control of your life. Visualize yourself as being powerful, able to tackle difficulties easily, and able to master whatever you choose. You are a superhero of your own making. Your special power comes from being you. Work, no problem. Friends, no problem. Lovers, no problem. You can do anything that you want, accomplish anything you try. Visualize yourself receiving the promotion you want, making a perfect swan dive, painting a masterpiece, and finding a compatible lover. Relish the feeling of power, of being able to take charge rather than being a victim. See yourself overcoming any obstacles in your life. Feel the strength and certainty that you can do anything you wish.

ENJOY THE TIME YOU SPEND ALONE.

It's nice to realize that time spent by yourself provides a space where you can have complete control over what you do without compromising your wishes or needs for anyone else. If the space starts feeling lonely, try to fill it with an activity that you especially enjoy, one that really gives you pleasure. Do you love to read, take bubble baths, watch sports on TV? It doesn't matter what you choose, just pick something that makes you feel good.

If filling the empty space with a favorite activity doesn't work, enlist a friend or family member to help you out. Remember, though, that you are ultimately your best company. You'll always be there for yourself, you know just what you like, and there's no one to argue with!

Passing Through the Indifference Stage

Alex had a disastrous ending to a relationship with Grace, a coworker from his office. His pain was exacerbated by the fact that he had to face her every day. His work fell apart because he worried constantly about bumping into Grace or what the other people in the office were saying about him being dumped. Alex finally requested a transfer to another section and used the space to work on resolving the termination of the relationship. A year later, he felt quite differently.

INTERVIEWER: How do you feel about things now?

ALEX: At this point, I can't even believe I felt so weird about the whole thing. I bumped into Grace in the elevator about a month ago. I didn't even have a reaction to her. In fact, she seemed a little put out that I didn't, which made me laugh. After we broke off I worried so much about whether I would run into her that my heart would start pounding and my hands would get sweaty any time I had to go into any of the central areas of the building. I guess I'm over that now.

INTERVIEWER: What do you think helped you to stop having a reaction?

ALEX: I don't know. I guess I went on with my life. I like my new assignment, and the people I work with are fun to be around. I've gotten into an exercise program at a nearby gym. I guess I've just put things into their place instead of making such a big deal over them. But I don't think I'll get involved with someone from the office again.

INTERVIEWER: Could you work with Grace now or be friends with her?

ALEX: I think I could work with her. I don't really think I would want to be friends with her. I don't like how she acted at the end. I don't know if she is the type of person I'd want to be friendly with. Maybe that's why she doesn't bother me so much now. Maybe I can just see her for who she is, and the person that she is doesn't really impress me.

Alex's entry into the indifference stage allowed him to get on with his life and begin to develop the skills for working toward a new relationship.

6

Growth

By this time, you have successfully come to terms with your old relationship. You have accepted what happened, dealt with it, and hopefully learned from it. You feel stronger and more integrated, ready to move on with your life. There's a new confidence present that enables you to approach your work, play, and social life with less hesitation and more enjoyment. Your doubts about your self-worth have diminished, and you have renewed faith in your ability to evaluate other people. The possibility of developing a new relationship seems less stressful and, at times, even enticing.

Barbara has changed considerably from the emotionally distraught woman of the preceding stages.

INTERVIEWER: How are things going for you now?

BARBARA: I've been doing well, actually. I was made supervisor of the clinical staff at work. It's been stressful at times, but I've really enjoyed the challenge. It's very different from just dealing with patients. I have to keep everyone at work happy and stimulated while handling conflicts and covering the workload. I feel like a juggler at times, but it's stretched me professionally.

INTERVIEWER: How are things in your personal life?

BARBARA: There's been a real change there as well. I started dating a few months ago. At first I was a little scared. With each person I met, I found myself thinking about whether I was getting into another bad situation. Eventually I stopped worrying about it and just concentrated on enjoying myself. There's been one special person lately, and that's been nice.

INTERVIEWER: Have you noticed any difference between the person you are now and who you were during the beginning of your relationship with Nick?

BARBARA: I think I was much more cautious in the beginning of this relationship. I didn't throw myself into my feelings right away and that actually created some problems. Paul, my new friend, felt that I was holding back, that I didn't trust him. Things got better when he told me how he was feeling, and I was able to let him know that I had been through a rough breakup and was a little wary of being hurt again. Paul promised he would be honest with me, and while I appreciated that, I still had reservations. I think it has meant a lot that he understood and didn't try to pressure me for a quick commitment. It made me feel valued. I also felt really good about owning my feelings and being able to communicate them without falling apart. It seemed that I could handle any outcome that came from my actions as long as I was clear about what I wanted, and I was proud that I didn't immediately collapse and give in to his wishes. I was able to take my own needs into account and hold firm.

Strategies for the Growth Stage

The growth stage is a time for trying out the lessons you have learned, a launching of the "new" you into interpersonal waters. Because you now feel comfortable with your own independence, you can consider balancing it with a relationship with someone else. Renewed intimacy is seen as an extension of your status as a whole human being.

Your goals for this stage should be:

⁊

Enjoy Yourself.

Develop New, Positive Relationships.

⁊

ENTER INTO A BRIDGE RELATIONSHIP.

Often when people return to dating after the termination of a bad relationship, they are very nervous about getting burned again. This causes them to be overly critical or fearful of potential partners since they're afraid of making another bad mistake.

It's often helpful to get involved in a bridge relationship until the perfect person comes along. This is a transitional relationship whose primary purpose is enjoyment, without any of the pressures of looking for your ideal mate. Choose someone who's passionate, makes you feel good, and wants to have fun. Work to keep the relationship on this level, and remember that there is another person involved. Be very clear about your feelings. You'd want someone to be honest with you; make sure that this person knows exactly where he or she stands at all times.

The bridge relationship will take the pressure off you—you know this isn't the person you are going to be with forever, so why get nervous or worried? It should also help you learn to keep interactions with people on a level that *you* determine. Best of all, it will give you a well-deserved good time!

THANK YOUR SUPPORTERS.

Chances are your friends and family have been through quite an ordeal as well. Why not thank those people who were there for you whenever you needed them? Take them out to dinner to celebrate your reemergence into life or do something especially nice just for them. Take some baked goods to the office. Make sure you let everyone know how much they have helped you and how grateful you are for their love and support.

KEEP AN EYE ON YOURSELF.

Value the changes you've made, the things you've worked through. As you return to dating, make sure that you don't slip into old patterns. It's important to review your options and not to limit yourself. Now is the time to enjoy your full potential and reap the rewards of all the hard work you've done. Take the time to evaluate your life. Are you still "new and improved"? Have you started to fall back into old behaviors that you don't wish to have? Make a deliberate attempt to review your performance so that your old habits don't creep back in.

OPENLY EXPRESS YOUR FEELINGS TO YOUR FAMILY AND FRIENDS.

It's important to practice positive emotional communication, particularly when you haven't had a chance to do it in a while. Use your friends and family as a sounding board. Practice ways of communicating love, anger, displeasure, and excitement with them. For instance, if you noticed that in your past relationships you always swallowed your anger, practice expressing displeasure when a family member does something you don't like. It's a safer place to try out new behaviors and you can ask them how your actions made them feel. It may be that they respected what you said, or it may be that you were too harsh. Work on fine-tuning your reactions so that you express exactly what you want in the manner you choose.

GO ON A VACATION.

Getting away is always fun. In this case, you can use the trip as a symbol of separating your old life from your new one. Visualize the vacation as a transition. When you return, you will be ready to let go of the past and start a new future. Don't forget to enjoy yourself while you're away! Reward yourself for all your hard work.

DEVELOP FORGIVENESS FOR YOURSELF AND YOUR OLD LOVER.

The final act of letting go often involves forgiveness. No matter how badly he or she treated you, your ex-lover has ultimately contributed to making you the strong, independent person you are today. That doesn't mean that you have to accept your ex-lover's actions—just forgive them and let go. If you don't forgive your ex-lover you stay tied to him or her. It is only by pardoning the past that you can free yourself to enjoy the future.

The same holds true for yourself. You might have acted badly in the past, shown poor judgment, or done things you might have preferred not to do. But look at how you've grown and changed, the progress and healing you've experienced. It's important to value yourself and forgive yourself for all of the previous pain. You are now ready to move on!

Passing Through the Growth Stage

Dean returned for his senior year of college feeling strong and relaxed. His breakup with Tess in the beginning of summer had been fairly traumatic. Eventually, the drama passed, and they were now able to be friends, which was probably a good thing since Tess was in several of his classes. Dean had spent the last two weeks of vacation surfing, enjoying his sense of freedom, and clearing his mind for the academic year ahead.

Of primary importance was his upcoming law school entrance exams, although his attention to his studies didn't stop him from having a decent social life. After a hard day of hitting the books, Dean liked going out with his friends to the movies or to dance clubs. He also enjoyed spending some of his free time with Jennie, a classmate of his who was a lot of fun. Jennie was pursuing her own academic path and didn't want to get seriously involved with anyone at this time. Dean found that being with Jennie enabled him to practice being responsive to a woman without slipping into the overprotective, smothering patterns that had destroyed his relationship with Tess.

Afterword

❧

Having a lover leave you can be a difficult and painful experience. There aren't many people who have escaped the ordeal. If there's some comfort, it lies in knowing that the feelings that emerge and the reactions you go through are fairly common. What is important is to withstand them and to emerge healthy and whole at the end.

Each of the stages that occur following the termination of a relationship serve some function. Realize that feelings will come and, with time and some hard work, transform into something else. Remember, if you find yourself becoming stuck at any level, work on the exercises for that stage. If they still don't help, seek outside help from friends or professionals. At the end of the experience you'll find the strength and confidence to meet life and love again.

This interview shows how Dorothy, a woman who had

been in a long-term relationship, managed to get through each of the stages successfully.

INTERVIEWER: What can you tell us about how your relationship began?

DOROTHY: Jerry and I met at an environmental rally about twenty years ago. We got along right from the start; perhaps it was our shared view of the world. We moved into a small apartment near the college where I was teaching. Jerry was working on a book at the time. Life was simple but romantic. We loved each other and the causes we both worked for. We never got married because we felt it was an unnecessary legal bond, but we were very much a couple.

INTERVIEWER: How long did you stay together?

DOROTHY: We were together for fifteen years, but only the first ten were really good. After that time, we started growing apart, our interests and focus began to change. Jerry started to drink more than I felt was good for him. I suppose he thought that I began to nag more than he felt was good for him. We still lived together, but we didn't share a lot of our time. I had more in common with a group of women friends and spent most of my free time with them. Jerry spent most of his free time isolated and drinking. He didn't care that I liked to go out often, and never minded if I did. It only became an issue when I wanted him to go with me.

INTERVIEWER: So how did you separate?

DOROTHY: Well, given Jerry's level of inertia, you can imagine my surprise when he sat me down one day and told me he wanted to leave. He said that he felt he was suffocating in our relationship, that it made him feel lazy and old. I was stunned. It's not that we had so much going for us or that I hadn't toyed with the idea of separation myself, but it was still a shock to hear him say that he wanted to split up.

INTERVIEWER: What did you do?

DOROTHY: I took a day and sort of holed up. Slept a bit and cried on the phone to friends. Once I recovered from the initial blow to my ego, I tried to get him to reconsider. I suggested going into therapy together to try to work it out. I told him that I knew I nagged him too much, and I would stop. I sensed that I hadn't been paying a lot of attention to my appearance over the past five years, so I started taking more care with how I looked. But he still said, no, he wanted to leave, to start a new life without me. I really got angry then. I mean, I had virtually spent fifteen years of my life with him, had put all my energy into making our relationship as good as it was, and was now being told I wasn't good enough. I was furious at this alcoholic lump telling me that I wasn't important enough to fight for.

INTERVIEWER: So what did you do?

DOROTHY: Well, I packed up all of my things and left. Every time I thought about what had happened, I'd get absolutely furious. I found the only thing that could calm me down was making pottery. I loved the feeling of the clay and the energy I expended making something out of nothing. I would pour all of my anger into the piece I was creating, and it didn't care. (Laughs) I guess I was throwing pots in a positive way: on the wheel, instead of at Jerry's head.

I spent a short time with a friend of mine, which didn't help matters, because she would talk to me about how I should be enjoying my new freedom and what a wonderful step this would be in my personal development. I know she meant well, but it wasn't what I wanted to hear right then. I finally found a house to rent and moved in, but I didn't have the energy to fix it up. I would just sit on the floor in the middle of all the boxes I couldn't unpack.

INTERVIEWER: What kept you from doing things?

DOROTHY: I was depressed, and I felt disembodied somehow. All of the context that had made me who I was for fifteen years had been removed. Even though I hadn't actively done things with Jerry for the past five years, he was part of my life, a framework for who I was. I felt kind of lost, and I obsessed on what I could have done to have made it turn out differently.

INTERVIEWER: What brought you out of this?

DOROTHY: It wasn't immediate, but I started doing more things. I've never been a person who could sit still for long, and I began to get active. I attended meetings and concerts and tried being really good to myself. I also realized that I wasn't any more lonely than when I was in that dead-end relationship, and that I liked being able to do what I wanted without having to feel guilty about Jerry being home by himself. I also began to see myself as someone in my own right, not as either "Jerry's woman" or "Jerry's reject." As a matter of fact, I didn't really feel connected to him in any way.

INTERVIEWER: Have you found anyone else?

DOROTHY: I've met some interesting people. I've found that I am able to take people for what they are and who they are, because I'm feeling very comfortable with myself. I have this sense that when I want to commit again, I'll do it happily.

Dorothy emerged from her relationship a stronger, more fulfilled woman, although there were moments during some of the stages when she probably didn't feel this would be the case. By continually working to get herself better, Dorothy adjusted to her separation and forged a new life.

Final Comments

You have been through a terrible ordeal. Don't let anyone tell you otherwise. While most everyone has been left by a lover, the experience is never as strong as when it happens to you. The following is a summary of the stages you have passed through on your journey to personal growth.

- Shock—You were devastated when your lover told you that the relationship was over. You couldn't believe that your dreams for a future together were shattered. Your senses shut down and you had difficulty eating or sleeping. You were able to move out of this stage by seeking comfort and protection while restoring your body, mind, and spirit.

- Hope—During this stage you tried desperately to reinstate the relationship. You wanted your lover back with you out of familiarity, loneliness, or pain. In working through this stage, you realized the importance of accommodating yourself rather than your ex-lover.

- Anger—In this stage, you became furious at your ex-lover, the relationship itself, and the way it had ended. Gone was the idea of winning your lover back; you wanted revenge. You passed through this stage by learning to vent your anger in a constructive rather than a dangerous way.

- Despair—No longer angry at your lover, you turned on yourself. You questioned your self-worth, and it was difficult to think or act positively. You worked through this stage by releasing the past and becoming more future-oriented. Instead of blaming yourself, you found constructive solutions to your problems.

- Indifference—Eventually, you realized that you weren't linked to your lover emotionally. You began to ask yourself questions such as "Where do I go from here?" You began to pave the path to independence and build the foundations for future relationships.

- Growth—You finally shed that person who occupied so much of your emotions and time. From this perspective, it almost seems unbelievable that he or she caused you so much distress. You are now ready to move into a more rewarding, positive relationship. Or you might have made the decision to enjoy life independently for now.

Growth doesn't occur in an hour or a day. But by being gentle and supportive with yourself, you can make the transition from pain to recovery. We hope you have found the suggestions in the book useful. Please remember, if you ever feel desperate or find yourself stuck at any stage, seek help. It's all right to get assistance; asking for support when you need it is actually a sign of inner strength.

Good luck.

RICHARD G. WHITESIDE AND FRANCES E. STEINBERG have spent the past twenty-five years working with relationship issues and family difficulties. Rick received his master's in social work followed by post-graduate training at the internationally acclaimed Family Therapy Institute of Washington D.C. He stayed at the Institute for ten years, teaching and supervising therapists, in addition to working in his own private practice. He is the author of *The Art of Using and Losing Control.* Frances received her Ph.D. in psychology from The Johns Hopkins University and has worked in a variety of settings including the University of New Mexico, rape crisis centers, and private practice. She is the author of numerous professional publications and the book, *Games Babies Play.* In 1994, Rick and Frances moved to Auckland, New Zealand, where he is Clinical Coordinator of family therapy training and clinical programs for Waitemata Health and she directs the Piha Healing Arts Centre. Together, Frances and Rick have co-authored *Whispers from the East.*